Skills for OU Study

Reading and Taking Notes

The Open University Walton Hall, Milton Keynes MK7 6AA

Edited, designed and typeset by The Open University.

Printed in the United Kingdom by Thanet Press

ISBN 978-0-7492-1266-7

1.1

Skills for OU Study

Reading and Taking Notes

Knowing how to read effectively and when to take appropriate notes can help you make swift progress during your course.
This booklet accompanies the *Skills for OU Study* website
http://www.open.ac.uk/skillsforstudy/, which contains advice, quizzes and exercises to help you improve your assignments.

Contents

1 Overview

Reading, listening and thinking as part of your Open University study often go hand in hand with taking notes of some kind. You will find that there are many different ways of reading and many different way of noting things down. Depending upon your situation, you might read things in greater or less detail, or you might focus on one particular section of a book. You might find yourself taking extensive notes, jotting down a few words, drawing diagrams or even taking no notes at all.

Many students find that the nature of what they are reading or listening to determines what type of notes they take. For example, if you are trying to outline complex relationships, a visual method of note taking, such as a mind map or systems diagram, might be the best way.

You might find yourself taking extensive notes, jotting down a few words, drawing diagrams or even taking no notes at all.

At the same time, you might find that your approach to your course materials (whether they be books or audio-visual material) changes according to what you need to achieve at that point in your course. For example, if you want to gather evidence from several different sources, you might not read all of those sources in great detail but scan them for relevant bits. However, if you need an understanding of a complex argument that one particular author is making, you might need to focus intently on that text.

Try to retain a flexible approach to your studying technique and be aware of your purpose whenever you prepare to read, watch or listen to anything for your course. You will come across different techniques in this booklet. Try a few of them out. Not all of them may be to your liking but you might find some of them useful in your studies.

2 Reading and listening

Reading and listening to academic material is very different from reading and listening for pleasure. It requires you to think actively about the material. For certain subjects, you may need to analyse and critique it, rather than simply absorb it as 'the truth'.

Some of what you read and listen to may be very densely worded and cover complex concepts or theories. You may also find that there is a great deal of material and you will need to find ways of coping.

> ❛ The glare of the white page was a real strain. I found that using a piece of coloured transparent plastic really helped my eyes. ❜

Do try to retain a flexible approach to your reading strategies and be aware of your purpose as you study. Some reading and listening materials may require more of your time than others.

There may be times when you have to acknowledge that you simply can't cover everything. If you discover this, don't panic! Try to reach a decision on what you *will* read and listen to and how much time you will spend on it. Talking to your tutor, study adviser or your OU regional centre will help you develop a strategy for coping with the work you have to do.

 Visit www.open.ac.uk/skillsforstudy for useful advice on reading strategies and techniques.

2.1 Your strategy

You may be surprised at how much material you need to read and watch on your course. Think about what your purpose is and what strategy you will use whenever you read anything. If you are busy, you might need to adopt a fast-reading technique in order to find relevant material. However, if you need to read something in detail, you should be prepared to slow down and use critical reading methods.

Use the learning outcomes for your course to focus your reading strategy.

Look at your course materials to find the learning outcomes for your course or for the particular block you are studying and use these to focus your strategy. You might also find that you don't need to look at all the materials you receive. Check your course guide to see if some of them are optional.

Staged approaches

When you really must absorb the information or when you're finding the content difficult, adopting a 'staged' approach to your reading might help. One such staged approach is SQ3R – a five-step approach to reading more effectively (see Figure 1). Although you may not always want to adopt SQ3R fully, you might find some of the steps useful. They are: survey, question, read, recall, review.

1 Survey – before you plunge in, look at the structure of the material (are there headings, diagrams, tables that might be useful to you?)

2 Question – try questioning what the material is about. Ask yourself: Who? What? Where? When? Why? How? If your course gives you questions to contemplate while reading or listening to the material, keep those close to hand.

3 Read (or listen) – try to read and listen in a relaxed but focused manner. Don't make notes if it gets in the way of your understanding.

4 Recall – test your memory of what you've just read or listened to. Jot down what you can remember without looking at the text.

5 Review – go back to the text and read it again, this time taking brief notes. Imagine how you might explain what you've read to someone else.

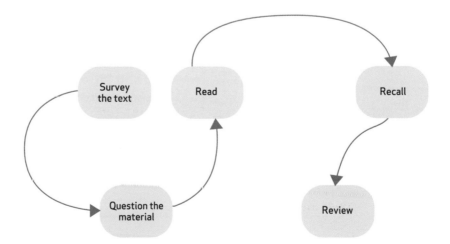

Figure 1   The SQ3R technique. Just one way of ensuring that you are reading your course materials effectively

The 'stop-review' technique may also help you undertake your reading. This involves reading in short bursts and using questions to review what you have just read. You can either use the questions listed below or write more appropriate questions of your own.

- What is (are) the key idea(s)?
- How much do you need to remember?
- How much detail do you need to note down?
- Do you have an opinion on what is being said? (… if it is appropriate to have an opinion.)
- How would you make it clear in your notes what is your own opinion?

Stop after you have read a couple of paragraphs and use your questions to guide you as you make notes. Then read on using the same technique.

2.2 Active reading

OU course materials are constructed to encourage you to read actively. For example, many texts have learning outcomes for each chapter or section. Keep these outcomes in mind as you read, and take time to review them once you've finished studying the material. Assessment is often closely tied to learning outcomes.

> ❛ I just couldn't seem to take the words in. I must have read the same piece several times. ❜

Course books often incorporate self-assessment questions that encourage you to reflect on what you have just read. Likewise, the audio and visual materials are constructed to engage your critical faculties as you watch and listen.

Aim to read and listen to everything in an engaged fashion. It is too easy to listen or read something passively and find that it has not registered in your memory. There are various strategies for ensuring that you are concentrating. One is to have a particular aim in mind as you read, for example, 'I want to find out how this theory is treated by this person' (see Section 2.1, Your strategy). Another is to try to apply what you are reading to things that are already familiar to you, either from earlier parts of your course or from your life, to gain a better understanding of the issue.

Aim to read and listen to everything in an engaged fashion.

Above all your aim should be to actively construct an understanding of the material you are reading.

2.3 Reading critically

Your course will include a variety of material from different sources. Try to approach all of it with an objectivity that allows you to distinguish well-supported arguments from unsubstantiated opinion. You may be required to critique some of the material you are presented with. Learning to read things with a critical approach will also help you to reflect on how you might produce strongly supported arguments of your own.

> ‘ I concentrated so hard on my reading that all of my effort seemed to be on the act of ‘concentration’ and not on actually thinking and interpreting what I was reading. ’

The aims of the text and what it hopes to establish can often be most easily identified at the beginning of the passage and in its conclusion. You could also try reading the back cover of a book or the acknowledgement page: these might give you some background on the author.

Use questions to help you examine material critically. This approach is particularly valuable for material that is not peer reviewed (that has not passed before an editorial panel of experts before being published). You can employ these critical questions on newspaper articles, internet sources and books. However, they are also useful when reading peer-reviewed materials, such as your course materials and journal articles.

Use questions to help you examine material critically.

Some guiding questions for your reading

Who is speaking or writing?

What is their point of view or perspective?

What ideas and information are presented and how were they obtained?

Are there unsupported assertions?

Are relevant reasons or evidence provided?

Is the method used to find the evidence sound? (e.g. with regard to sample size or control group where statistical significance is claimed)

Is the evidence correct or valid?

What assumptions have been made?

What is fact and what is opinion?

What are the implicit and explicit values?

Are there unreasonable generalisations?

What has been omitted?

How were the conclusions reached?

Are the conclusions reasonable?

What other perspectives or points of view could there be?

2.4 Evaluating online material

When evaluating material that you find online, you should engage in the same critical questioning as with paper-based material. Many of the online texts that you look at will be electronic versions of published journals and books. However, some online material might be in the form of blogs, wikis and other websites, where information is presented in a different way and you might need to search a little harder for evidence that it stands up to critical scrutiny.

- Analyse as you read – do the arguments hold together? Do the facts tally? Try thinking about the content in the following terms.

- Relevance – the purpose of the website might be very different from your purpose in studying your course.

- Objectivity – be aware of whether the author is arguing from a particular perspective. A bias to the writing might not necessarily rule the material out of your studies, but you should highlight and acknowledge it when quoting or paraphrasing.

- Supporting evidence – are assertions based on evidence that is traceable to a reliable source, or on information that you know to be reliable? Try not to be influenced by a well-worded or passionate exposition that isn't systematically argued and backed up with evidence.

- Other influences – has the work been sponsored by an organisation that might have influenced the interpretation of the results? Alternatively, the site might be sponsored by a reputable organisation, which might encourage you to have greater confidence in the information you find there.

- Provenance – where does the information come from? Look for an 'about this site' page that tells you about the authors of the site and their aims. Look at the web address: if it ends in '.ac.uk' it belongs to a university in the UK.

- Timeliness – is the site kept up to date, or does it look abandoned? There is often a copyright date and symbol somewhere on the site that indicates when the material was produced or when it was last updated.

- Method – if you are looking at a research report, are the methods used for data collection and analysis clear?

 Visit the OU electronic library at http://ltssolweb1.open.ac.uk/safari/signpost.htm to see more on searching for and evaluating information.

2.5 Fast reading techniques

There may be times when you need to get through a lot of material in a short space of time. Fast-reading techniques (such as scanning and skimming) can help you to quickly find the useful parts of the texts you need to read. If you skim or scan something and decide that it's not worth reading closely, you've saved yourself some valuable time. If you find that the material is useful, however, you will need to slow your pace down and start looking a little closer at the text.

Fast-reading techniques can help you to quickly find the useful parts of the texts you need to read.

Although these two techniques have been described separately here, you may find yourself skimming and scanning a piece of writing simultaneously.

Scanning

This is useful when you want to quickly extract some specific information from a text but you don't want to have to read the entire text (see Figure 2). Scanning an article or book enables you to pick out words or phrases without having to go into the broader meaning of the text. If you are looking for something particular, try scanning the page for specific words, phrases or acronyms. These words should jump out at you as your eye moves down the page.

You can also try this technique on the contents list, index or illustration list to see if key words appear there. You can ignore what the book or article is trying to say and simply concentrate upon the words you want to find.

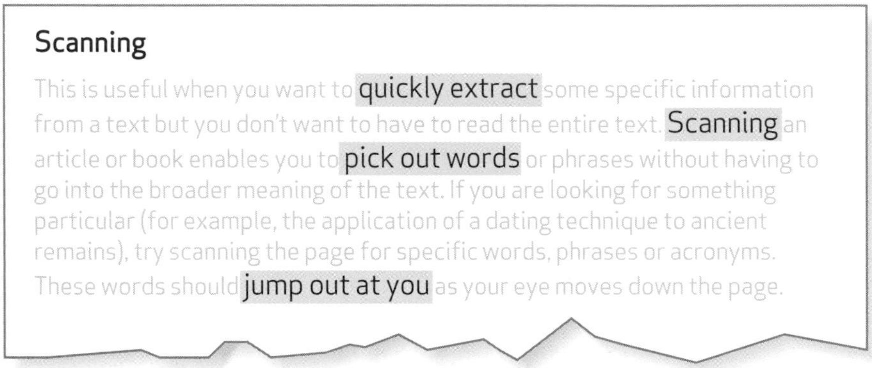

Scanning

This is useful when you want to **quickly extract** some specific information from a text but you don't want to have to read the entire text. **Scanning** an article or book enables you to **pick out words** or phrases without having to go into the broader meaning of the text. If you are looking for something particular (for example, the application of a dating technique to ancient remains), try scanning the page for specific words, phrases or acronyms. These words should **jump out at you** as your eye moves down the page.

Figure 2   As you scan the text your eye will pick up on certain words and phrases

Skimming

Skimming, in contrast, involves reading sentences quickly to find the main ideas of the material you are looking at (see Figure 3). This type of reading doesn't leave you with a complete comprehension of the material you've read, but it helps you to obtain the main point very quickly. You don't have to read every single word. Allow your eyes to skim over the sentences and you will find that you quickly pick up on words that give you clues to what the text will say next.

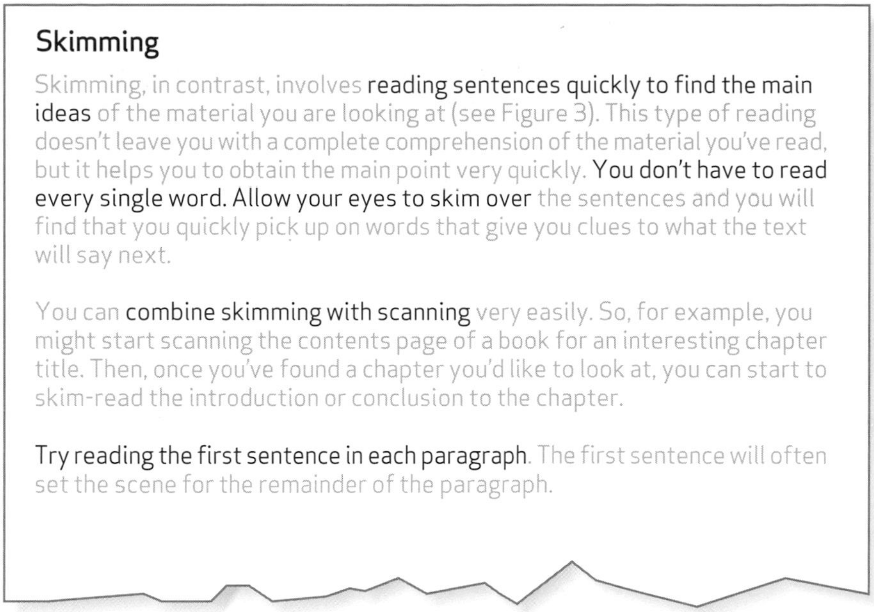

Skimming

Skimming, in contrast, involves reading sentences quickly to find the main ideas of the material you are looking at (see Figure 3). This type of reading doesn't leave you with a complete comprehension of the material you've read, but it helps you to obtain the main point very quickly. You don't have to read every single word. Allow your eyes to skim over the sentences and you will find that you quickly pick up on words that give you clues to what the text will say next.

You can combine skimming with scanning very easily. So, for example, you might start scanning the contents page of a book for an interesting chapter title. Then, once you've found a chapter you'd like to look at, you can start to skim-read the introduction or conclusion to the chapter.

Try reading the first sentence in each paragraph. The first sentence will often set the scene for the remainder of the paragraph.

Figure 3   Allow your eyes to skim quickly over the text so that you come away with the gist of the material

You can combine skimming with scanning very easily. So, for example, you might start scanning the contents page of a book for an interesting chapter title. Then, once you've found a chapter you'd like to look at, you can start to skim-read the introduction or conclusion to the chapter.

Try reading the first sentence in each paragraph. The first sentence will often set the scene for the remainder of the paragraph.

Other fast reading tips

- Look at the introduction: it might give you a useful overview of the chapter or article.
- Skip straight to the conclusion and read that quickly.
- Look at the contents list to discover the overall structure of the book.
- Look for signpost words (such as: essentially, most importantly, in conclusion) to help identify the most relevant parts of the text.

2.6 Reading complex material

From time to time you will come across course material that is complex. Don't panic if this happens. It is only to be expected that at university level you might struggle to comprehend some of the texts. There are strategies that you can adopt to help you tackle this problem.

Don't plunge straight into the material. Quickly flick through to get an idea of the structure.

- Don't plunge straight into the material and try to wrestle some meaning out of it. Step back and try a few simple checks first. Quickly flick through to get an idea of the structure of the piece. Do headings and sub-headings indicate the direction of the text? Are there any helpful summaries? Are there any illustrations that help to explain what is meant by the text, such as diagrams or tables?

- Try to identify the difficulty by analysing what the text covers – for example, what particular aspect of a topic it is focusing on and what has it left out? You could also find another book that covers this topic that might explain it in a way that will help you understand.

- Use a good general dictionary and, if you can find one, a specialist dictionary for your discipline. There are some useful electronic dictionaries available from the OU's online library website (http://library.open.ac.uk/). Specialist dictionaries explore the vocabulary of your subject and focus on concepts, theories and people that are important (for example, a social sciences dictionary will have an entry on Michel Foucault). They don't simply give you synonyms of words but may explore a term, phrase or concept more fully.

Try piecing together what you do understand.

- Write down what you *do* understand. Sometimes a gap can be filled by piecing together what you do understand. Try using the 'stop-review' technique of reading (see section 2.1) where you read in short bursts of a couple of paragraphs before stopping and writing notes. Even if you are not sure that you understand the material, trying hard to write down what you *think* someone else is trying to say is sometimes a good way of working out a difficult argument.

- Don't give up too soon. If you carry on reading, you may find a piece of the puzzle that helps you understand the overall text. You might have to accept that you can't understand something at the moment, but that you can come back to it later on, once you've gained an understanding of related subjects.

Online forums are often useful for getting help.

- When all else fails, always remember that there is someone you can ask for help: another student or your tutor or study adviser will try to explain it to you. Online forums are often useful for getting help and you might find that someone has raised the query there already.

3 Why take notes?

Taking notes can contribute to the process of active reading and, therefore, help you focus on the topic you're studying. If you are selective in the techniques you use for taking notes you can tailor them to specific purposes – for example, to collect together material from across the course that will be helpful when you come to revise for an exam or work on an assignment.

3.1 Develop good habits

Try to develop good note-taking habits from the start of your studies.

Always write your notes in your own words.

- Always write your notes in your own words. Don't simply copy down the exact words that you are reading. By translating what you are reading into your own words you stand a better chance of properly understanding what it: you internalise the meaning of the material.

- Be aware of the risks of plagiarism. If you do copy material word for word, rather than use your own words, be sure to note the source so you can acknowledge where it comes from if you quote from it in an assignment. Accessing reading material online makes it very easy to highlight and copy blocks of text into your documents and then forget that it is not your own work. When you submit assignments, you will be expected to confirm that the work is all your own.

Write down where the ideas in your notes have come from.

- Write down where the ideas in your notes have come from: the book or chapter, the page, the journal title, the article title, or whatever is appropriate. If you have noted down a direct quotation from someone, always put the page number the quotation came from, otherwise you'll spend time looking for it again later on. If you are taking notes from a website or blog, make a note of the website address, the name of the website and the date on which you accessed it. You are expected to create a reference list of your sources at the end of your assignments.

- When you find a perfect quotation, make sure that you put obvious quotation marks around the words in your notes (when you come back to your notes perhaps months later, you will have forgotten whether you or someone else wrote the words unless you make it obvious with quotation marks).

3.2 Your strategy for taking notes

There is no one correct way of taking notes. Different situations require different approaches so always bear in mind the purpose of your reading and listening. Sometimes you might need to make comprehensive notes of a full text. At other times you might feel that just a few scant notes and a precise quotation are required. Sometimes you might feel that you simply need to write a few marginal notes in the course book itself (a very useful technique).

> 6 It was only when I had to tackle the essay question that I realised I hadn't really got enough from my reading, despite all my notes. 9

So think about the material when choosing what sort of notes to take. For example, a visual technique, such as a mind map or a systems map, might be best to help you represent complex relationships, while tabulated notes might help you make a direct comparison of different theories.

But most importantly, you should always think about your purpose.

- What your notes are for? Are they intended to summarise a broad range of key course materials? They might be used to prepare you for an assignment, or you might be reworking old, longer notes to create, more concise notes for an exam.

- What type of material are you are taking notes from? Is it a chapter containing an overview that requires detailed notes, or a chapter from which you only need small bits of information? You might need to scan the article or chapter before deciding to take any notes.

3.4 Organise your notes

Find a way of organising your notes with meaningful labels, well thought-out categories and colour coding.

Once you've started to take notes, you'll find that they quickly expand and you need to find a way of organising them so you can find what you want later. There are some common factors to well organised notes: meaningful labels, well thought-out categories, colour coding.

Filing paper notes

If you hand write your notes, find a way to keep your papers in order. Some students like to use a lever-arch file, ring binders or concertina files. Get hold of useful things like sticky labels and plastic folders.

- If you use a lever-arch file you can use dividers to classify your notes. Try labelling these and listing the headings in an index at the front.

- If you use a concertina file use sticky labels to categorise each compartment.

- Colour coding using highlighters or sticky labels can help you quickly find what you are looking for. For example you could use green for material on theories, yellow for case studies and red for the names of key writers in your field.

Organising computer files

Think about how best to organise the documents and files you create on the computer. Make sure you set up a folder structure with meaningful labels.

If you lose a file on your PC, type its name into Windows Explorer to search for it. There are also some useful and free applications on the internet (for example, Google Desktop and Yahoo) that will index your files and allow you to search all files on your computer.

Use a portable storage device such as a pen drive to carry your files around with you.

A portable storage device such as a pen drive (flash disk or memory stick), can be very useful if you work on more than one computer, so that you can carry your files around with you wherever you go. Be careful how you name your file each time you save it so you don't lose track of which is the most recent.

Make sure you have a system to back up your computer files. Use a CD, a separate hard drive or another storage device to keep the latest version of your files.

 Visit http://www.open.ac.uk/skillsforstudy/ to find out more about using your computer to organise your folders and files.

3.5 Techniques for taking notes

There are many ways of taking notes, for example:

- Text-based notes: writing notes in your course books, creating tables with notes in, creating summary cards.

- Visual notes: drawing mind maps, systems maps, line diagrams or using highlighters and coloured stickies to colour-code existing notes.

- Audio notes: using a computer or digital recorder to create audio that you can listen to later on.

You can also combine these different practices and create some very powerful notes. You will find more information on these techniques below. Each has its strengths and weaknesses. Some may appeal to you more than others, but do try out some different techniques to see when they work best for you.

If you prefer to make notes on your computer rather than by hand, you will be able to find free software packages online. These range from electronic index cards and mind mapping software to websites where you can store your documents.

 Visit http://www.open.ac.uk/skillsforstudy/ to find out more about techniques for taking notes.

Highlighting, annotating and coloured stickies

While some might find the idea of writing in their text books difficult at first, many students find it a useful technique, and OU texts are often designed with a wide 'scholar's margin' for this purpose.

Using the restricted space in the margins of your course books encourages you to process the concepts, theories or processes you are reading about and reword them as a short précis (see Figure 4). Being able to paraphrase concisely and accurately is an important writing skill that will stand you in good stead for assignments and exams.

The visual aspect of writing in your course books and highlighting is important and you will find it much easier to scan the material when you return to it later on. Using coloured highlighters enhances this visual impact and it can also be helpful to colour code parts of the text. However, be careful not to overdo it, as too much highlighting becomes distracting and might indicate that you aren't really studying the text effectively.

You can also write notes on coloured stickies and use them as bookmarks, or stick them to the wall of your study area.

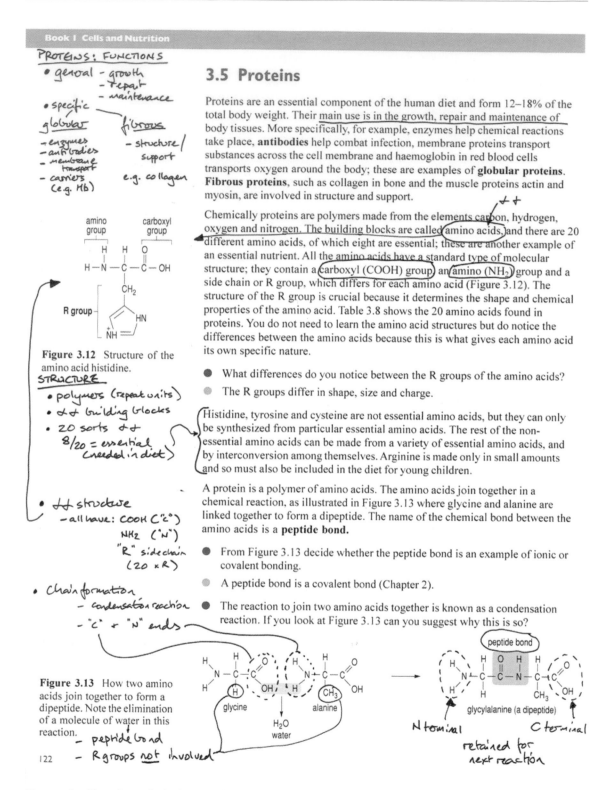

Book 1 Cells and Nutrition

Handwritten margin notes (left):

PROTEINS: FUNCTIONS
- general - growth
  - repair
  - maintenance
- specific
  globular   fibrous
  - enzymes   - structure/
  - antibodies   support
  - membrane
    transport
  - carriers   e.g. collagen
    (e.g. Hb)

amino group   carboxyl group

Figure 3.12 Structure of the amino acid histidine.

STRUCTURE
- polymers (repeat units)
- ++ building blocks
- 20 sorts ++
  8/20 = essential
     (needed in diet)

- ++ structure
  - all have: COOH ("c°")
             NH₂ ("N")
             "R" side chain
             (20 × R)

- Chain formation
  - condensation reaction
  - "c" + "N" ends

Figure 3.13 How two amino acids join together to form a dipeptide. Note the elimination of a molecule of water in this reaction.
- peptide bond
- R groups not involved

122

3.5 Proteins

Proteins are an essential component of the human diet and form 12–18% of the total body weight. Their main use is in the growth, repair and maintenance of body tissues. More specifically, for example, enzymes help chemical reactions take place, **antibodies** help combat infection, membrane proteins transport substances across the cell membrane and haemoglobin in red blood cells transports oxygen around the body; these are examples of **globular proteins**. **Fibrous proteins**, such as collagen in bone and the muscle proteins actin and myosin, are involved in structure and support.

Chemically proteins are polymers made from the elements carbon, hydrogen, oxygen and nitrogen. The building blocks are called amino acids, and there are 20 different amino acids, of which eight are essential; these are another example of an essential nutrient. All the amino acids have a standard type of molecular structure; they contain a carboxyl (COOH) group and amino (NH_2) group and a side chain or R group, which differs for each amino acid (Figure 3.12). The structure of the R group is crucial because it determines the shape and chemical properties of the amino acid. Table 3.8 shows the 20 amino acids found in proteins. You do not need to learn the amino acid structures but do notice the differences between the amino acids because this is what gives each amino acid its own specific nature.

● What differences do you notice between the R groups of the amino acids?

◐ The R groups differ in shape, size and charge.

Histidine, tyrosine and cysteine are not essential amino acids, but they can only be synthesized from particular essential amino acids. The rest of the non-essential amino acids can be made from a variety of essential amino acids, and by interconversion among themselves. Arginine is made only in small amounts and so must also be included in the diet for young children.

A protein is a polymer of amino acids. The amino acids join together in a chemical reaction, as illustrated in Figure 3.13 where glycine and alanine are linked together to form a dipeptide. The name of the chemical bond between the amino acids is a **peptide bond.**

● From Figure 3.13 decide whether the peptide bond is an example of ionic or covalent bonding.

◐ A peptide bond is a covalent bond (Chapter 2).

● The reaction to join two amino acids together is known as a condensation reaction. If you look at Figure 3.13 can you suggest why this is so?

Handwritten notes on Figure 3.13:
peptide bond
glycine   alanine   glycylalanine (a dipeptide)
H_2O water
N terminal   C terminal
retained for next reaction

Figure 4   Use the scholar's margin in your course books to jot down notes

	Biological	Families	Cultures
Key researchers	Mednick and others	Chicago School Shaw and McKay	Clarke and Coleman
Causes of crime	Genetic predispostion	Generational transmission of criminal careers in problem families	Zones of transition favour male gang sub-cultures; crime not seen as normative problem.
Evidence	Twin studies Adoption studies	Longitudinal studies	Geographical surveys Participant observation
Weaknesses	Corporate crime? Social assumptions?	What is good parenting? Role of education, class, culture?	Cultures without gangs? Role of economics?

Figure 5   Tabular notes can help you structure the relationships between things such as theories, concepts or authors

Tables, glossaries and lists

Creating tables, either on paper or on the computer, can help you sort through relationships between concepts, important authors, processes and other things. For example, a table might help you compare the different facets of three contrasting theories (see Figure 5).

You could add arrows and draw images to indicate relationships or strengths and weaknesses.

Making lists under headings can help you to order your notes into groups, and alphabetical glossaries are a great way of keeping track of any specialist terminology for your course.

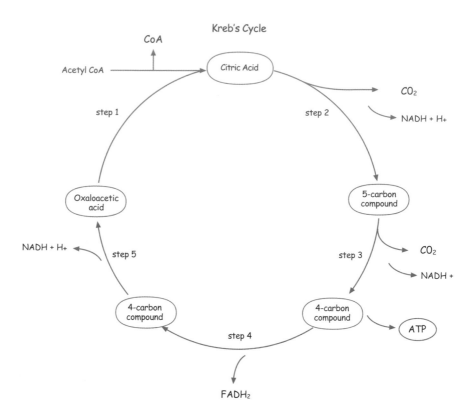

Figure 6   A line diagram of the Kreb's cycle

Line diagrams

Line diagrams (such as flow diagrams) are very useful for the visual representation of logical progressions, such as stages in a process, or for complex relationships. For example, biology students might use a line diagram to indicate the different stages of the Kreb's cycle (see Figure 6).

Keep the number of words to a minimum in order to make the most of the visual strength of the diagram – just use trigger words or phrases rather than full sentences. You can add longer written notes below the diagram to supplement your understanding. You could also use coloured highlighters on these notes.

Mind maps

Mind maps are another visual method of taking notes, also known as spray notes, concept maps or patterned notes. They show how different aspects of a subject relate to one another. Whereas line diagrams use arrows to show a progression or process, mind maps

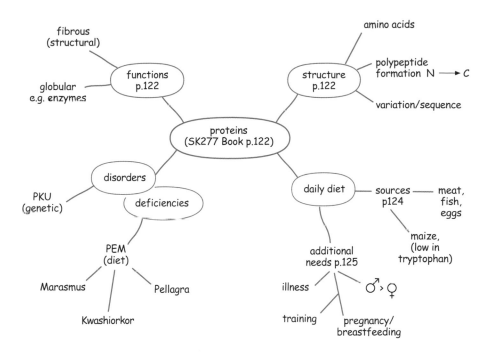

Figure 7   This mind map condenses a long description of proteins from the second level OU course, Human Biology (SK277)

are like a snapshot of the often complex relationship between concepts and ideas (see Figure 7).

As with line diagrams, you should use words or succinct phrases in your mind map rather than sentences, and you can add colour and symbols.

Free electronic mind maps are available to download from the web. They are easy and quick to use and can be used to produce some very effective study notes.

Systems maps

Like mind maps, systems maps can capture a snapshot of a complex relationship. They are particularly good at demonstrating overlapping relationships between different components of the map (see Figure 8 overleaf). The process of drawing a systems map can help you think through the structure of a subject and commonalities and relationships between different elements. Dotted lines can be used to indicate tentative boundaries between subsystems.

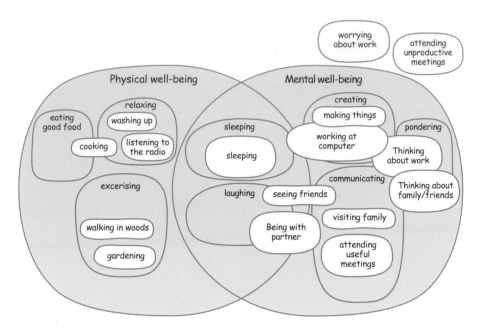

Figure 8   Complex and overlapping relationships can be represented very effectively with a systems map

Summary cards

Writing notes on index cards can be an effective way of summarising. Using a combination of words, colours and drawings, you can create a highly organised set of memory aids that will be of use later on when you are facing an assignment or exam (see Figure 9).

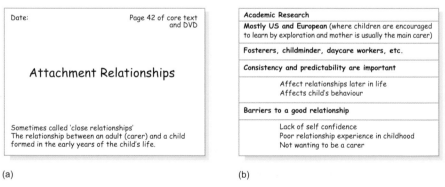

(a)   (b)

Figure 9   Summary cards (a – front of the card, b – back of the card). It is up to you how you organise your notes on your summary cards

Electronic index cards have added benefits, such as search mechanisms to allow you to find keywords. Free software applications have more elaborate versions that you are expected to pay for.

Audio notes

Some students find that they learn well from audio notes. You could use a digital voice recorder, an iPod or a mobile phone to create audio notes that you can listen to when you choose.

Go to http://www.open.ac.uk/skillsforstudy for more information on how to use iPods and other devices to record your notes.

Taking notes from spoken material

OU study often involves watching and listening to course material. You may be expected to listen to audio CDs, watch filmed interviews and lectures, and have face-to-face sessions with a tutor.

In all these situations you need to develop strategies for dealing with a continuous flow of information from the speaker: to identify the most important bits of the flow as it happens and write notes quickly while continuing to listen for the next important fact.

Although you can stop and replay recorded materials, try not to do this too much or your note taking process will become very time consuming. Don't do a full transcription of what you are listening to – be disciplined with yourself and take shortened notes. If you do want to write down a quotation, remember to use quotation marks and write down the details of where the quote came from.

There are many things you can do to become more efficient at listening to and making notes from spoken materials.

- Brief yourself on the subject before you listen

- Use abbreviations in your notes

- Leave white space in your note pad for later, additional notes

Gather some information before you start listening. If your course materials contain notes to accompany the programme, read those first so that you get the gist of the interview, lecture or programme. If you are going to a tutorial, your tutor may want you to read certain units of your course before the tutorial starts. This preparation helps to focus your listening and help you anticipate what might be coming up.

Remember to record the date and any other relevant information at the top of your notes and if you need to check on something that you might have missed in the lecture, ask your tutor or a fellow student after the tutorial.

Using abbreviations when you write can help you cope with the speed at which you need to take notes while listening to someone. There are established abbreviations but you can also make up your own. If you already know shorthand, you are lucky!

When you take notes in a hurry you may find that you want to return to certain parts of your notes later on to add to them. Try to leave lots of space on the page around your paragraphs or bullet points as you take your notes.

Making notes on formulae and problem solving

Maths courses often use problem-solving tasks as a way to help you learn formulae. These tasks help you practice your problem-solving skills and apply those skills to both familiar and unfamiliar situations. These tips will help you as you work through these tasks.

- Don't erase your notes if you've made a mistake. Simply put a line through the part of the formula that is wrong, put a line underneath it and recommence your notes underneath that. When you are working your way through calculations, your mistakes can actually help you eventually achieve the right answer.

- Leave plenty of white space around your workings so that you can make additional notes later on if you need to.

- Problem-solving tasks, and learning maths generally, may involve proceeding in a step-by-step fashion, so work through calculations and problems thoroughly: don't try to find shortcuts or to jump over any of the stages.

Sharing your notes

You might benefit from finding a group of like-minded fellow students with whom you can share notes. Looking at other people's notes can help you clarify things that you might not have understood.

Some websites allow you to keep your notes online. These websites often have the facility to make your stored notes public to everyone (sometimes this is the default), or available to selected individuals. Other benefits of these websites might be the ability to link to other online encyclopaedias and glossaries (such as Wikipedia), to organise your notes easily, set yourself reminders and format your notes so that they are easier to read.

 Visit www.skillsforstudy.open.ac.uk to see a selection of these websites.

One benefit of using these websites to make and keep your notes is that you don't have to worry about losing them. Even if your computer breaks down or if you lose your memory stick, the notes that you keep on the website will remain safe.

Reworking your notes

The notes you take during your course will provide a resource that you can rework for other purposes, for example for assignments and examinations. Reworking notes also gives an opportunity for revision, as you have to go back through the thinking process again as you rework them. You might even find yourself keeping these notes for reference in future study.

- When reworking notes for an assignment, keep the assignment question with you to help focus your attention. Look for guidance from your assignment guide, which might prompt you to look at certain areas of your course materials to answer a particular question. If you have filed your notes well, you will be able to go straight to the relevant material.

- When you rework your notes for an exam, you will probably find yourself reducing the length of your older notes. As you read them try to condense them and then use these second generation notes as your revision material.

4 These skills will take you forward

It takes everyone time to find the best way to read, understand and take notes at university. Don't worry if you don't feel efficient at first. Allow yourself a little time to get used to different ways of taking notes and get to grips with the difficult course materials.

Most importantly, don't be reticent about asking for help. If you don't understand something, your tutor or study adviser can to point you in the right direction. You may find that a little clarification on a particular sentence or paragraph is all you need – recognising when you need help and knowing how to ask for it can save you a great deal of time and anxiety and is a good skill to cultivate in itself.

Do take the skills of note taking and effective reading seriously. You will find that time spent on developing your skills now will improve your ability to cope with the demands of study in the future. The skills involved in being an efficient and effective student are immensely useful in other areas of your life too, for example in the work place. Develop those skills now and you'll never look back.